CELEBRATE THE UNITED STATES!

WHY DO WE HAVE NATIONAL HOLIDAYS?

BY BEATRICE HARRIS

Gareth Stevens PUBLISHING

Please visit our website, www.garethstevens.com. For a free color catalog of all our high-quality books, call toll free 1-800-542-2595 or fax 1-877-542-2596.

Library of Congress Cataloging-in-Publication Data
Names: Harris, Beatrice, author.
Title: Why do we have national holidays? / Beatrice Harris.
Description: New York : Gareth Stevens Publishing, [2026] | Series: Celebrate the United States! | Includes index.
Identifiers: LCCN 2024052387 (print) | LCCN 2024052388 (ebook) | ISBN 9781482471038 (lib. bdg.) | ISBN 9781482471021 (paperback) | ISBN 9781482471045 (ebook)
Subjects: LCSH: Holidays–United States–Juvenile literature.
Classification: LCC GT3933 .H384 2026 (print) | LCC GT3933 (ebook) | DDC 394.26973–dc23/eng/20250118
LC record available at https://lccn.loc.gov/2024052387
LC ebook record available at https://lccn.loc.gov/2024052388

Published in 2026 by
Gareth Stevens Publishing
2544 Clinton Street
Buffalo, NY 14224

Designer: Jeffrey Taylor
Editor: Therese Shea

Photo credits: Series art (blue background) Paladin12/Shutterstock.com; Cover, p. 1 Africa Studio/Shutterstock.com; p. 5 M_Agency/Shutterstock.com; p. 7 AI Generated/Shutterstock.com; p. 9 AI Generated/Shutterstock.com; p. 10 (inset) nestudio99/Shutterstock.com; p. 11 Jen Wolf/Shutterstock.com; p. 13 Sheila Fitzgerald/Shutterstock.com; p. 15 Ringo Chiu/Shutterstock.com; p. 17 Glynnis Jones/Shutterstock.com; p. 19 Bastiaan Slabbers/iStock.com; p. 21 Limolida Design Studio/Shutterstock.com.

Printed in the United States of America

CONTENTS

Times to Remember 4
Birthdays 8
Independence Day 12
Remembering Those Who Serve 14
Newest National Holiday 18
A Few More 20
Glossary 22
For More Information 23
Index 24

Boldface words appear in the glossary.

Times to Remember

Do you like birthdays? They are a special day to **celebrate** someone. The United States has 11 special days called national holidays. Some are happy days. Others are more **serious**. Some are both! Americans should know what each day means.

The **federal** government has national holidays so the whole country can celebrate. How people celebrate can be different from place to place. The kind of celebration also depends on the holiday. Many businesses close so workers can enjoy the holidays with their families and friends.

CLOSED
4 th july

Birthdays

Some national holidays honor people. George Washington was a general in the **American Revolution**. He was the first U.S. president too. Washington's Birthday is a national holiday celebrated on the third Monday in February. Many call it Presidents' Day. They honor President Abraham Lincoln too.

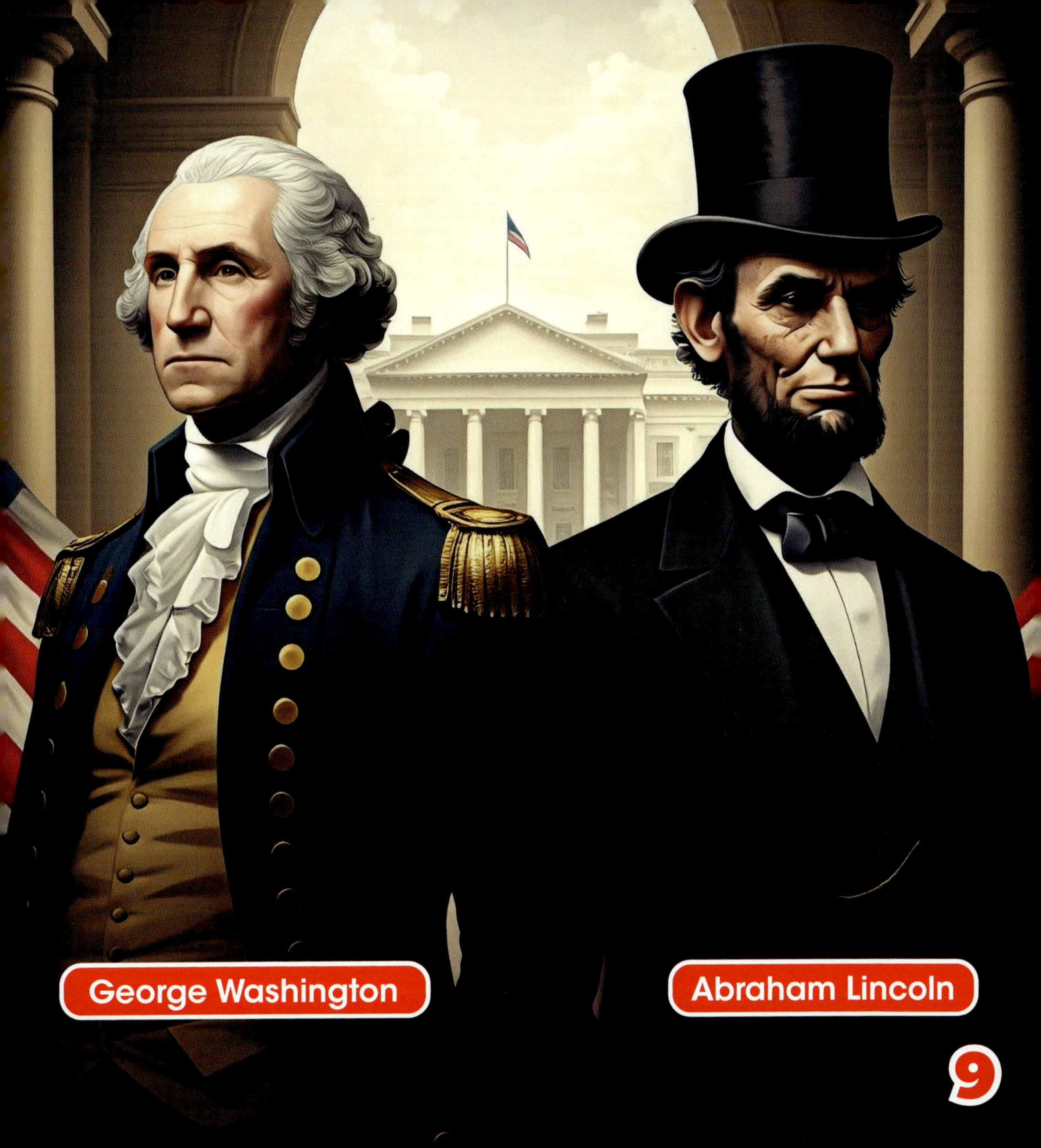
George Washington
Abraham Lincoln

The U.S. government honors Dr. Martin Luther King Jr.'s birthday on the third Monday of January. King was an important leader in the **civil rights movement**. Many people do acts of service to hono King on Martin Luther King Jr. Day.

Dr. Martin Luther King Jr.

Independence Day

Independence Day is a birthday for the United States! It celebrates the birth of the country on July 4, 1776. That's the day the Declaration of Independence was approved. The Declaration announced the American colonies were independent, or free, from British rule. Today, people celebrate with parades and fireworks.

PIZZA BAR
15

Remembering Those Who Serve

Some holidays honor soldiers. Memorial Day is a day to remember all U.S. soldiers who have died in wars. On the last Monday in May, many people visit **cemeteries** to show respect for soldiers who gave their lives for their country.

MVP
MERGING VETS & PLAYERS
ROAR

On November 11, Veterans Day is a national holiday to honor everyone in the U.S. armed forces. It's a time to give respect to those who serve the country. People in the military **sacrifice** a lot for their country. This is a great day to say, "Thank you!"

know
NYC
district

Newest National Holiday

The newest national holiday is Juneteenth National Independence Day, on June 19. It became a federal holiday in 2021. Juneteenth celebrates the end of slavery in the United States. People celebrate with prayer services, **picnics**, and **festivals** of dancing and music.

A Few More

There are even more national holidays! Labor Day celebrates workers. Columbus Day honors Christopher Columbus landing in the Americas in 1492. New Year's Day, Thanksgiving, and Christmas are three more national holidays in the United States. Which holiday is your favorite?

Know Your National Holidays

Name	Day
New Year's Day	January 1
Martin Luther King Jr. Day	third Monday in January
Washington's Birthday	third Monday in February
Memorial Day	last Monday in May
Juneteenth National Independence Day	June 19
Independence Day	July 4
Labor Day	first Monday in September
Columbus Day	second Monday in October
Veterans Day	November 11
Thanksgiving Day	fourth Thursday in November
Christmas Day	December 25

GLOSSARY

American Revolution: The war in which the colonies won their freedom from England.

celebrate: To honor with special activities.

cemetery: A place where the dead are buried.

civil rights movement: A time period in U.S. history starting in the 1950s in which Black Americans fought for equal civil rights, or the freedoms granted to us by law.

federal: Having to do with the national government.

festival: A special time or event when people gather to celebrate something.

picnic: A meal eaten outdoors.

sacrifice: To give up something, which allows someone else to receive something.

serious: Dealing with matters in a thoughtful way, not trying to be fun or funny.

FOR MORE INFORMATION

BOOKS

Kaul, Jennifer. *Our Traditions: What Symbols and Celebrations Do Americans Share?* New York, NY: DK Publishing, 2023.

Lynch, Seth. *Celebrating Juneteenth.* New York, NY: Cavendish Square, 2023.

WEBSITES

American Holidays

www.usa.gov/holidays
Read more about federal holidays and other important days around the country.

Celebrating Juneteenth

kids.nationalgeographic.com/history/article/celebrating-juneteenth
Read about the long history of our newest holiday.

Publisher's note to educators and parents: Our editors have carefully reviewed these websites to ensure that they are suitable for students. Many websites change frequently, however, and we cannot guarantee that a site's future contents will continue to meet our high standards of quality and educational value. Be advised that students should be closely supervised whenever they access the Internet.

INDEX

American Revolution, 8

armed forces, 16

Columbus, Christopher, 20

Declaration of Independence, 12

federal government, 6

Juneteenth, 18

King, Martin Luther, Jr., 10

Lincoln, Abraham, 8

soldiers, 14

Washington, George, 8

wars, 14